WRITING EFFECTIVE E-MAIL

Improving Your Electronic Communication

Nancy Flynn and Tom Flynn

A FIFTY-MINUTE™ SERIES BOOK

Crisp Learning.com

Menlo Park, California

WRITING EFFECTIVE E-MAIL
Improving Your Electronic Communication

Nancy Flynn and Tom Flynn

CREDITS
Managing Editor: **Kathleen Barcos**
Editor: **LuAnn Rouff**
Production: **Barbara Atmore**
Typesetting: **ExecuStaff**
Cover Design: **Fifth Street Design**

© 1998 by Crisp Publications, Inc.
Printed in the United States of America by Von Hoffmann Graphics, Inc.

CrispLearning.com

00 01 02 03   10 9 8 7 6 5 4

Library of Congress Catalog Card Number 98-71224
Flynn, Nancy and Tom Flynn
Writing Effective E-Mail
ISBN 1-56052-515-0

This book is printed on recyclable paper with soy ink.

LEARNING OBJECTIVES FOR:

WRITING EFFECTIVE E-MAIL

The objectives for *Writing Effective E-Mail* are listed below. They have been developed to guide you, the reader, to the core issues covered in this book.

Objectives

- ❑ 1) **To discuss planning and composing e-mail messages**

- ❑ 2) **To suggest effective presentation and mechanical techniques of e-mail**

- ❑ 3) **To discuss managing and organizing e-mail**

Assessing Your Progress

In addition to the learning objectives, CrispLearning has developed an **assessment** that covers the fundamental information presented in this book. A twenty-five item, multiple choice/true-false question-naire allows the reader to evaluate his or her comprehension of the subject matter. An answer sheet with a chart matching the questions to the listed objectives is also available. To learn how to obtain a copy of this assessment, please call **1-800-442-7477** and ask to speak with a Customer Service Representative.

Assessments should not be used in any selection process.

DEDICATION

*Nancy Flynn dedicates this book to her husband, Paul Schodorf,
whose generous gift of editing expertise and time made it possible,
and to her children, Bridget and Tim.*

Tom Flynn dedicates this book to his loving wife, Sammi.

*We thank our parents, Dorothy and Lou, for instilling in us an appreciation
for well-written books. And we are grateful to Crisp Publications'
Phil Gerould for making this brother-sister writing team's book a reality.*

ABOUT THE AUTHORS

Nancy Flynn is founder of the E-Policy Institute™, an organization devoted to helping employers limit e-risks through the development and implementation of effective e-mail, Internet, and software policies. Through the E-Policy Institute, Ms. Flynn conducts Electronic Writing Workshops, Netiquette Programs, and E-Policy Seminars for corporations, associations, and government entities. Recognized for her expertise in the areas of electronic communication and e-policy development, Ms. Flynn has been featured by the *Wall Street Journal, Woman's Day,* National Public Radio, and other national media outlets. In addition to *Writing Effective E-Mail*, Ms. Flynn is the author of *The E-Policy Handbook* and *The $100,000 Writer*. For more information on safe and effective electronic communication, visit www.ePolicyInstitute.com.

Tom Flynn is Senior Information Systems Project Leader for Liebert Global Services. Mr. Flynn has been working with midrange, mainframe, and personal computer systems since 1982. Mr. Flynn is fluent in numerous software development languages and has a wide range of experience with several varieties of e-mail software. His e-mail address is tpflynn@netset.com.

A workshop based on the material presented in this book is available from Nancy Flynn's E-Policy Institute™. Please contact Ms. Flynn for information:

Nancy Flynn, Managing Director
E-Policy Institute
2300 Walhaven Ct. Ste. 100A
Columbus, OH 43220

Toll Free: 800-292-7332 Phone: 614-451-8701 Fax: 614-451-8726
E-mail: nancy@ePolicyInstitute.com
Website: www.ePolicyInstitute.com

CONTENTS

CONTENTS (continued)

INTRODUCTION

E-mail is rapidly becoming the most common—and quickest—means of business and personal communications. Just because e-mail gets there faster, however, does not mean you should spend less time sweating the mechanical details. All business correspondence—whether written on a screen or traditionally on paper—projects an image of you and your organization.

An e-mail document full of grammar, punctuation and spelling errors will tax the reader's patience and lessen your credibility. In the battle for the reader's on-screen attention, carefully written e-mail that is free from mechanical errors is sure to come out on top.

Evaluate Your Current Writing Skills

Your ability to write a clear, concise, nonelectronic message the good old-fashioned way will determine the effectiveness of your e-mail documents. The following self-assessment will help you evaluate your attitude toward electronic writing, identify your writing strengths and weaknesses, and focus your electronic writing efforts more clearly.

EXERCISE

	TRUE	FALSE
1. Because e-mail is intended and expected—to be a quick, informal means of communication, the usual rules of grammar, punctuation and style don't apply.	❏	❏
2. You can enhance the readability and impact of your e-mail message by using all uppercase (or all lowercase) letters.	❏	❏
3. Short sentences indicate intellectual weakness. You are certain to impress readers by writing long, heavily punctuated sentences.	❏	❏

EXERCISE (continued)

	TRUE	FALSE
4. Always save the best stuff for the end. If you reveal the most important information up front, the reader will have no incentive to finish reading your document.	❏	❏
5. Electronic writing is fundamentally different from traditional writing.	❏	❏

Score:

5 False: You are well on your way to becoming an effective electronic writer.

4 False: Remember, good writing is good writing, regardless of whether it's produced on paper or on a screen.

2–3 False: Before you begin writing, focus on your goal. As a writer, your primary job is to persuade the reader. It's hard to persuade someone who can't understand what you are saying.

1 False: A comprehensive grammar and punctuation review may be a good idea. Focus particularly on Parts III and IV of this book.

ANSWERS: 1. False; 2. False; 3. False; 4. False; 5. False

ASSESSING YOUR COMPUTER SKILLS

Before addressing the specifics of effective electronic writing, you may want to take a few minutes to evaluate your computer skills. Once you determine your current level of expertise, and understand where you want to go, achieving your communications goal will be easier. If you already have a clear idea of both how you want to use e-mail and what skills you need, skip to Part I, "Before You Write Your E-Mail Message."

1. Ask yourself, *"What do I want my computer to help me do?"*

    - Are you a hobbyist who wants to send e-mail to friends, play electronic games or surf the Net?

    - Are you interested in using your computer to perform business functions such as writing letters and memos, creating spreadsheets, and communicating with coworkers, vendors and customers?

    - Are you a *power user* who designs and writes computer programs or works with complex mathematical, scientific and/or statistical applications?

2. Make a detailed list of your professional and personal tasks and interests. For each item, indicate how a computer might help you. This list will help you shop for computer equipment and software. It also will help you organize and manage your computer's use:

TASKS AND INTERESTS   **YOUR COMPUTER'S ROLE**

(1) _____   (1) _____

_____   _____

_____   _____

(2) _____   (2) _____

_____   _____

_____   _____

(3) _____   (3) _____

_____   _____

_____   _____

ASSESSING YOUR COMPUTER SKILLS (continued)

3. As part of your self-assessment, test your grasp of *Computer 101* basics:

   What does the CPU do? _____

   What is the purpose of a modem? _____

   What is CD-ROM? _____

   How is a diskette used? _____

4. Do you understand the difference between hardware and software?   ❑ Yes   ❑ No

5. What size computer do you need to accomplish your goals?

   _____

6. Do you know how to find *help* information on your computer?
   ❑ Yes   ❑ No   On your software?   ❑ Yes   ❑ No

7. Do you know how to make back-up copies of your work?
   ❑ Yes   ❑ No

8. Do you understand the basic functions of the software you are using?   ❑ Yes   ❑ No

Improving Your Computer Skills

When it comes to computers, there is always more to learn. If, after completing your self-assessment, you feel the need to brush up on the basics, help is available:

► Search online booksellers, retail bookstores or the library for publications that answer questions at your level. Most publishers are sensitive to the needs of beginning, intermediate and advanced computer users.

► Use the *help* facilities in your software. Save the manufacturers' manuals you receive when you purchase new hardware and software; they can be invaluable when problems arise.

► Seek the advice of friends, colleagues and family members who regularly use computers and are able to explain concepts in understandable terms.

► Take classes at your local computer store, community center, high school or university.

► Keep an open mind. Mastering difficult computer concepts and learning new electronic skills requires patience, persistence and a willingness to learn.

P A R T

I

Before You Write Your E-Mail Message

BEFORE YOU WRITE YOUR E-MAIL MESSAGE

While you may consider the message itself to be the most important part of your e-mail, there are some preliminary concerns to think about before writing. Is e-mail the best way to convey your information? If so, who is your audience? Should you send a copy (or blind copy) to anyone else? The following guidelines will help you answer such questions every time you consider writing an electronic message.

E-Mail in the Workplace

If your primary use of e-mail will be in the workplace, be aware that while e-mail may be the quickest form of written communication, it is far from the most secure. You may intend to send a confidential e-mail message to one person, but it's easy to hit the wrong key and accidentally send your message to dozens or hundreds of unintended readers. Your message can also be instantly forwarded by its recipient.

There's also a good chance *Big Brother* is reading over your electronic shoulder. According to the Society for Human Resource Management, more than 36 percent of employers peek at employees' e-mail, and over 70 percent believe it is the employer's right to read anything in the company's electronic communications system.*

Sexual harassment and other workplace lawsuits have resulted from employees writing and sending improper e-mail messages. Many people treat e-mail too casually, sending electronic messages they would never put on paper. Play it safe. Don't write anything to or about another that you would not feel comfortable saying face-to-face. If your organization has not developed a written e-mail policy, now is the time to do so.

---

* Society for Human Resource Management, "E-Mail Becoming a Workplace Norm, But E-Mail Policies Lag Behind, Survey Finds," Press Release, 8 February 1996. For additional information, visit SHRM on the Internet at www.shrm.org.

WHEN SHOULD YOU USE E-MAIL?

However you intend to use e-mail, don't rely on e-mail when a phone call or meeting is more appropriate. E-mail is quick and convenient, but it is not always the best means of communication. Opt for a telephone call or face-to-face meeting if the following circumstances apply.

► Your message is extremely important or confidential, and you can't risk a breach of privacy. If you aren't willing to have your words read by an unintended audience, don't use e-mail. It's simply not secure.

► You need to deliver unpleasant news and don't want to appear cold or indifferent. As a rule, deliver bad news in person or via the telephone. This gives you the opportunity to *warm up* your message with appropriate facial expressions, body language and vocal inflection. For example, e-mail would be the most effective way to notify the accounting department of a mandatory staff meeting. But the meeting itself—not a cold, impersonal e-mail message—would be the appropriate place to break the news that the department is being downsized.

► There is a chance your written message will be misunderstood.

► You need an immediate response. E-mail may be the best way to deliver news fast, but it is not necessarily the best route to a quick reply. For an immediate response to a pressing issue or question, use the telephone or meet face-to-face.

Before you write your first electronic word, think about your message and your intended reader. Consider any outside factors—such as language barriers, time zone differences and "hidden" readers—that could affect how your electronic message is received. Then decide whether or not e-mail is the way to go.

WRITING FOR INTERNATIONAL AUDIENCES

You can send an e-mail message across the continent or around the world as easily as you can communicate with your colleague in the next cubicle. Are you prepared for the cultural challenges of international electronic communication? Take this five-point quiz to see where you stand.

	YES	NO
1. Fundamentally there is no difference between international and domestic e-mail.	❏	❏
2. You don't have to worry about language barriers. English is, after all, the international language of commerce.	❏	❏
3. International e-mail calls for more detailed and specific information than does local e-mail.	❏	❏
4. All speakers of any given language are culturally similar.	❏	❏
5. When e-mailing a colleague in another country, it is all right to use technical jargon, acronyms and abbreviations.	❏	❏

Answers

1. *No.* Whether you are sending e-mail messages to extended family members in another country or business associates abroad, international communication poses unique challenges of language, culture and time. E-mail writers should think carefully about their readers' needs before writing and sending messages abroad.

2. *No.* When composing your e-mail message, don't assume your audience reads and understands your language. Know who your reader is before you begin to write. If necessary, have your message translated into the language(s) best understood by your audience.

WRITING FOR INTERNATIONAL AUDIENCES (continued)

3. *Yes.* Keep your message focused and your writing tight to increase your chances of being understood by international readers. Writing *Our video conference will begin at 6 P.M. on 3/7/99*, for example, could have disastrous results.

   Americans would read that date as March 7, 1999. Europeans would read it as July 3, 1999. And the Japanese, using a year/month/day order, would face more confusion. Because Europeans use a 24-hour military clock, be sure to write international e-mail according to that format. *Our video conference will begin at 6 P.M. on 3/7/99* becomes *Our video conference will begin at 18:00 on 7 March, 1999.*

   When sending domestic e-mail messages, be sure to indicate the time zone (Eastern Standard Time, *EST;* or Pacific Standard Time, *PST*).

   Measurements can prove equally challenging when sending e-mail abroad. To eliminate confusion, give the metric measurement, followed by its American equivalent in parentheses. For example, *Paul ran a 10-kilometer (6.2-mile) road race on Saturday.*

4. *No.* English-speaking Americans differ culturally from the English-speaking populations of Australia, Ireland and Canada. In fact, English-speaking Americans differ culturally from English-speaking Americans who live in other parts of the country and/or have different ethnic backgrounds. So too do Spanish-speaking Mexicans differ culturally from Spaniards and French-speaking Canadians differ culturally from the French.

5. *No.* Even if you are sending e-mail to an employee at one of your own company's international locations, never use acronyms, technical jargon, abbreviations or humor. Given language and cultural differences, there is too much opportunity for misunderstanding and confusion. And be specific. American terms—*Midwest* and *West Coast; jr. high* and *secondary school,* for example—are too vague for international readers who may not be familiar with the geography of the United States or who may live in a country with an educational system different from that of the United States.

ADDRESSING YOUR E-MAIL MESSAGE

Distributing e-mail is different from sending traditional mail through the post office (now called *snail mail*). With traditional mail, you simply address an envelope to each recipient, then drop the letters in a mail box. With e-mail, even the act of addressing a message takes forethought, as you have the option of sending the same message to one person or an entire group of readers.

Sending E-Mail to Individual Recipients

There are two ways to address messages to individual recipients:

1. *Write the Recipient's E-Mail Address on the Address Line Every Time You Send a Message.* A nice easy method if you rarely e-mail an individual, but inefficient when you repeatedly communicate with someone.

2. *Use an Electronic Address Book.* Almost all e-mail packages allow users to create an address book with the names and e-mail addresses of people frequently contacted. Simply select a name from your electronic address book and your software does the addressing work for you.

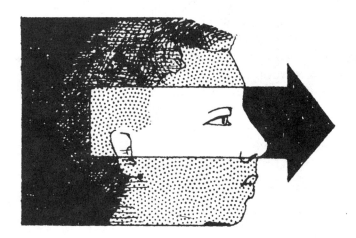

ADDRESSING YOUR E-MAIL MESSAGE (continued)

Reaching Multiple Readers

Most e-mail software allows you to send copies and blind carbon copies of your messages. Generally it's as easy as selecting *To, Cc* or *Bcc* when addressing your e-mail.

E-MAIL ADDRESS ELEMENT	DEFINITION
To	Use this option for the primary recipient(s) of your message.
Cc	*Cc* is shorthand for carbon copy. Enter the address of anyone you'd like to receive a copy of your e-mail on the *Cc* line.
Bcc	*Bcc* means blind carbon copy. If you want to send a copy of your e-mail without the original recipient's knowledge, put the address on the *Bcc* line.

Avoid controversy and hurt feelings by listing the last names of *Cc* recipients in alphabetical order.

Remember, just because it's possible to send carbon copies and blind carbon copies doesn't make it appropriate in all circumstances. Send carbon copies only to those who need to read your document. E-mail users are inundated with legitimate correspondence and junk mail. Sending a copy to someone who really doesn't need to read your message wastes everyone's time.

Blind carbon copies pose an additional challenge. Sent to the wrong person, a *Bcc* can cast an unfavorable light on the writer, who might be perceived as a troublemaker.

Using Group Lists

Many e-mail software packages allow you to create and maintain group lists. If, for example, you frequently send e-mail to the members of your project team, you could add their names and e-mail addresses to a group list labeled *project team.* When you want to e-mail the entire team, simply select the group name, and the addressing is completed for you.

Replying to a Message

At times, it may be more appropriate to reply to a received message, rather than write and address a brand-new one. Replying to a message is as easy as clicking on *Reply.* The original message will be displayed, with the *To* and *From* lines reversed and the addressing work completed.

Leave the original subject line intact, even if your reply changes the subject. Doing so provides continuity for the original writer and any intended and hidden readers you pick up along the way.

Add your reply above or below—*never within*—the original message. And always include a salutation and signature to ensure that your comments are identifiable, no matter how many times the message is appended and forwarded. If your software allows you to forward your reply to other readers, click *Forward,* write the new addresses on the appropriate *To, Cc* or *Bcc* lines, and then click *Send.*

ADDRESSING YOUR E-MAIL MESSAGE (continued)

Requesting a Receipt

Suppose you have written a crucial message that absolutely must be delivered. Short of receiving a response, how can you be certain your message has been received and read?

The quickest, easiest route to peace of mind is to select the *receipt notification* option on your screen. When the reader opens your message, you will be notified automatically. Many e-mail packages offer this feature. However, software incompatibility might inhibit notification.

A note of caution: Think about your reader before choosing the *receipt notification* option. Some readers may resent the implication that you don't trust them to open their e-mail.

Sending a Priority Message

Many e-mail packages allow you to assign *high, normal* or *low priority* messages. Not a means of speeding electronic delivery, the priority designation simply helps readers decide how quickly to read and respond to messages. Use the priority feature judiciously. If every message you send carries the *high priority* designation, readers will begin to disregard the label and question the importance of all your correspondence.

PART

II

Composing Your
E-Mail Message

COMPOSING YOUR E-MAIL MESSAGE

One of e-mail's greatest features is that you can communicate with just about anybody anywhere whose PC is equipped with e-mail software. One of the biggest challenges of e-mail is that once you send an electronic message, you usually lose control of it.

When you compose an e-mail message, don't assume your intended recipient will be the only person to read it. Mistakes happen. You could hit the wrong key and inadvertently send a private message to a group of readers. Or your intended reader could elect to forward your message to unintended or *hidden* readers.

Avoid problems and enhance communications with all readers—intended and hidden—by applying the five electronic communications rules on the following page.

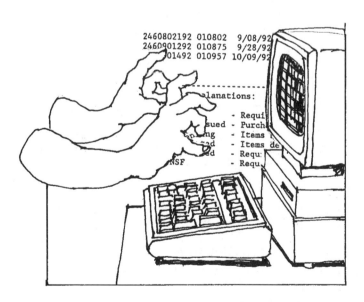

COMPOSING YOUR E-MAIL MESSAGE (continued)

Five Rules of Using E-Mail

1. **Write As Though Mom Were Reading.** Regardless of the intended reader, write to the widest audience imaginable. Be specific, but write your message as if your boss, the media or Mom were reading. If your message is too personal, confidential or important to write generically, reconsider e-mail as your vehicle.

2. **Think Big Picture.** Write specifically, even technically, if the situation calls for it. But always provide a brief executive summary at the beginning of the document. The executive summary serves two purposes: (1) Any reader, regardless of technical training, will understand your message; and (2) Because the executive summary is written in conversational language and appears at the beginning of the document, you stand a better chance of maintaining the interest of a reader who may not want to work through a complex, technical document.

3. **Keep an Eye on Spelling, Grammar and Punctuation.** You can be sure your readers will notice.

4. **Don't Use E-Mail to Let Off Steam.** If you are upset about something or angry at someone, take a few minutes to compose *yourself* before composing your message. Once you push *Send,* your e-mail is on its way through cyberspace and probably cannot be retrieved. If you are fuming, give yourself a 48-hour cooling-off period before writing and sending your e-mail message. As a rule, don't write anything that you would not be comfortable saying to the recipient's face. And never use obscene, abusive or otherwise offensive language. Your message could appear on the screens of hundreds, thousands, or even millions of hidden readers. Do you want all those strangers labeling you petty and irrational?

5. **Don't Send to the World.** E-mail users frequently complain about *spam,* the electronic equivalent of junk mail. Respect others' electronic space, as you would have them respect yours. Send e-mail only when appropriate and strictly to those who need to read it.

The following sections will help you compose e-mail that serves the purpose for which you intend it.

WRITING A SUBJECT LINE WITH *REAL OOMPH*

In the course of a business day, e-mail users may receive dozens, even hundreds, of messages. The battle to capture the attention and interest of the electronic reader is fierce. Part of your job as a writer is to ensure that your message is opened, read and acted upon.

Writing a subject line with *real oomph* can help you accomplish that task. Typically, a reader's e-mail inbox will display only the brief subject line of each message received. Writers often compose subject lines that are too vague, boring or cute to be effective. With a little effort, however, you can learn to write subject lines that make your e-mail messages stand out.

Tips for Writing Powerful Subject Lines

▶ **State Your Message Clearly, Concisely and Descriptively.**

A subject line that reads *Quarterly Results* does not have the impact of *Third Quarter Sales Up 15%*. A descriptive subject line draws the reader to the message by providing an accurate sense of what you have to say *before* the message itself is opened and read.

▶ **Consider Your Primary Audience When Writing the Subject Line, but Don't Overdo It.**

Resist the urge to use jargon, acronyms or technical terms, even if you are certain the reader will understand. You want to entice readers, not scare them away before they start reading.

▶ **Remember the Hidden Reader.**

When messages are forwarded from one reader to the next, the original subject line often is left intact. This gives you the opportunity to attract a broader audience of unintended readers to your message.

▶ **Don't Use the Subject Line to Oversell Your Message or Trick the Reader into Opening Your Document.**

A reader may fall for a misleading subject line once, but the next message you send might be ignored or deleted before it is read.

WRITING A SUBJECT LINE WITH *REAL OOMPH* (continued)

Serving Multiple Audiences with a Single Subject Line

To send a single message to many people with varying needs and interests, write a subject line that appeals to everyone.

Let's say your supervisor asks you send an e-mail memo inviting members of the accounting and information systems departments to a demonstration of a new accounting software package. If you write a subject line that reads *Accounting Software Demo*, the information systems department probably will assume the demo does not pertain to them and delete the memo without reading it. If, on the other hand, your subject line reads *Technical Perspectives of Accounting Software*, the accountants might be scared away.

The solution: Write a subject line that appeals to both audiences. *Vendor to Demo Accounting & Tech Aspects of New Software* might result in a solid turnout from both departments.

INCORPORATING A SALUTATION AND SIGNATURE

Because you never can be certain where your e-mail message will land—possibly on the screens of coworkers, supervisors, customers, vendors and others—it's advisable to incorporate a salutation and signature into the body of every important message. This allows hidden readers to follow your message's trail, mindful of the original sender and recipient. It's also a good idea to include a salutation and signature when you are forwarding messages. Identify your intended recipient; explain in a line or two why you are passing along the message; and sign your name. Doing so will establish your role in the electronic document's history, regardless of how many times it is forwarded.

Another benefit: Your signature signals the end of the message, sparing readers the annoyance of scrolling to the end of the screen to see if there is more copy.

Creating a Signature File

Many e-mail packages allow you to add a customized signature to all your messages, eliminating the need to re-enter copy each time. For example, you could add your company name and e-mail address to each message you send by creating a signature file that reads as follows:

> *Bridget F. Schodorf*
> *Schodorf Truck Body & Equipment*
> *bfschodorf@schodorf.com*

If you want, you can add a picture to your signature, using standard keyboard characters. Just remember to keep your signature picture appropriate to the message and audience.

Bridget F. Schodorf
Schodorf Truck Body & Equipment
bfschodorf@schodorf.com

GRABBING THE READER'S ATTENTION: THE LEAD

To maximize the impact of any written document—electronic or traditional—you must start strong. The lead—beginning with the first word of the first sentence and ending at the conclusion of the first paragraph—is the writer's best, and sometimes only, opportunity to grab the reader's attention.

A well-conceived lead draws readers in, motivating them to read the document through to its conclusion. If the lead is well-written, your reader will grasp your meaning right away, and decide immediately whether to continue reading, save your document for later review, or delete it.

Understanding Your Lead's Role

- The lead structures your message. The reader has no doubt why you have written it or whether to continue reading.

- The lead delivers the document's most important, compelling information right up front, often in the form of a conclusion.

- The lead summarizes what is to come later in the document.

- The lead captures—and holds—the reader's attention.

SAMPLE LEADS . . . WEAK AND STRONG

Here are two examples of weak leads, along with suggested revisions.

Weak Lead #1

Of LLF & Associates' 2,500 employees, approximately 2,000 are using the company's e-mail system on a regular basis. The problem is that many of the 2,000 persons enjoying the company's e-mail are using it for personal correspondence. Management is aware this is going on and wants it stopped. As of January 1, the e-mail system of LLF & Associates is reserved for business use. Any employee caught using it for personal reasons will be put on probation. Three violations of the new e-mail policy will result in termination.

ANALYSIS: This weak lead contains too much unnecessary and secondary information, all of which appears at the beginning of the paragraph. The reader does not learn until the final three sentences that the company is instituting a tough new e-mail policy.

Revised Lead #1

Effective January 1, personal use of LLF & Associates' corporate e-mail is prohibited. Employees who violate this e-mail policy by making personal use of the system will be put on immediate probation. Three violations will result in termination.

ANALYSIS: This strong lead tells readers what they need to know. A busy reader can grasp the message's meaning immediately.

SAMPLE LEADS . . . WEAK AND STRONG (continued)

Weak Lead #2

This is a response I have written to Gloria, who recently shared her thoughts about her concerns for our association and our board. I think she has raised important issues that we must address. I send it to you because Tim and I believe we absolutely need a strategic planning session no later than December.

ANALYSIS: The writer wastes valuable time describing the e-mail message to the reader (*This is a response I have written; I send it to you because*), rather than simply delivering the message. A well-written message should be strong enough to stand alone without any introduction.

Revised Lead #2

Tim, Gloria and I agree our association faces enormous challenges. Let's hold a strategic planning session by December to review board members' concerns and begin planning for the future.

ANALYSIS: At 29 words, this strong lead is nearly half the length of the 55-word original. Succinct and to-the-point, this lead conveys the writer's thoughts clearly and quickly.

EXERCISE

Rewrite the following weak lead, moving the most important information to the beginning.

Jane Tomm, a graduate of State University, with a master's in journalism and a bachelor's in English, is an integral member of the Health Department's public relations team, serving initially as a public information officer then as manager of special projects. An employee of the state for 12 years, Jane also has published two books of children's fiction and is a volunteer tutor with the city schools, teaching writing skills to high school students. Effective today, Jane has been named communications chief for the State Health Department. All supervisors, managers and staff will begin reporting to Jane immediately. Please plan to attend tomorrow's 7 A.M. staff meeting to learn more about Jane's promotion and her plans for the department.

USING THE INVERTED PYRAMID

Good business writing is structured as an inverted, or upside-down, pyramid. The most important information is communicated right up front, in the lead. Following the lead, information is presented in descending order of importance.

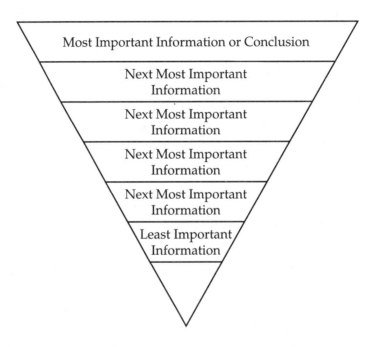

Why take an inverted pyramid approach to writing e-mail? Deluged with electronic and traditional correspondence, few business people have time to read every memo, letter and proposal that crosses their computer screens or lands on their desks.

How does a harried reader decide which e-mail documents to read and respond to, and which to delete from the screen? Typically the reader scans the lead—the first few words and sentences—and then decides whether to continue reading. This is why it is so important to deliver your primary message right up front, at the beginning of your e-mail document. Before writing, think about your goal. Do you want to alert readers to a problem? Notify your staff about a rescheduled meeting? Persuade your supervisor to increase your department's budget?

Whatever the objective, state your message clearly, concisely and as close to the beginning of your e-mail document as possible, ideally in the first sentence of the first paragraph.

ORGANIZING DOCUMENTS CHRONOLOGICALLY

The inverted pyramid is not the only way to organize e-mail documents, but it certainly is the best way to ensure your letters and memos are read and retained, before deletion from the screen. Many writers, unfamiliar with the inverted pyramid approach, format their writing chronologically. The problem with most chronological writing, however, is that it takes the reader too long to get to the *good stuff*. Consider, for example, this chronological letter from a college student looking for a post-graduation job:

Document with Chronological Format

Dear Personnel Manager:

My name is Matt Kennedy. I'm a 22-year-old college senior who will graduate from State University this June with a degree in English.

During my four years at SU, I served first as a writer for, then as the editor of, the university's literary magazine. In addition, as a junior, I was a sports columnist for SU's student newspaper, *The Beacon.*

My university-level editorial work was a natural offshoot of my experience at City High School. During my tenure at CHS, I was actively involved as a member of the school's yearbook and newspaper staffs.

It's no surprise that my academic career has focused so extensively on communications. I did, after all, publish my first book when I was a mere eighth-grader. Co-authored by my mother and published by Scribners, that fictional children's work is now in its second printing.

I would like to put my communications experience to work for XYZ Company. I hope you will consider me for an entry-level position in your public relations department.

Sincerely,

Matt Kennedy

ANALYSIS: This chronological letter is written in *mystery writer* style. Not until the final paragraph does the personnel manager learn what Matt wants. Matt gambles that the reader will stick with him to the end. Given the weakness of his lead and the boredom inherent in chronological writing, Matt is taking a big risk sending this e-mail letter to a busy personnel manager.

ORGANIZING DOCUMENTS CHRONOLOGICALLY (continued)

Document with Inverted Pyramid Format

Dear Personnel Manager:

Would a published author with eight years of experience as a writer and editor be a valuable addition to your company's public relations staff? If that communicator were a 22-year-old looking for an entry-level position to get his career off to a terrific start, would you be interested? I'm Matt Kennedy, and as you can tell, I have packed a lot of experience into the first two decades of my life. I'd now like to put that experience to work for XYZ Company.

A senior at State University, set to receive a bachelor's degree in English this June, I am seeking an entry-level position in XYZ Company's public relations department. What assets would I bring to XYZ?

1. **Professionalism:** I published my first fictional children's book in the eighth grade. Co-authored by my mother and published by Scribners, that book is now in its second printing.

2. **Teamwork:** I served on the staffs of SU's literary magazine and student newspaper. In high school, I worked on the yearbook and newspaper staffs. I understand how to work as a part of a team of writers, editors, designers and photographers.

3. **Leadership:** As the editor of SU's literary magazine, I developed a knack for motivating staff and an understanding of what it takes to complete a project on a deadline and within budget.

I hope to have the opportunity to meet with you in the near future.

Sincerely,

Matt Kennedy

ANALYSIS: This e-mail letter has *real oomph.* Matt makes it clear in the first two paragraphs that he is looking for an entry-level PR position. And thanks to his unique and powerful lead, he distinguishes himself from every other college graduate hoping to get a foot in the door at XYZ Company.

GETTING STARTED IN THREE EASY STEPS

For many people, the hardest part of the writing process is getting started. The thought of writing the first few words in the all-important lead sentence paralyzes many writers. Don't let a blank screen intimidate you. Apply this three-step trick for getting started.

1. Begin your lead sentence with a well-worn cliché such as *"The purpose of this memo is,"* or *"I am writing today because,"* or *"In response to your e-mail of April 1,"* or *"Thank you."*

2. Complete your first sentence by attaching your primary message to the cliché you selected to jump-start the writing process. Then continue writing your document, inverted-pyramid style.

3. When you are finished writing, return to the first sentence and replace your opening cliché with a stylish, attention-getting phrase. Make any necessary changes to the rest of the message.

The result: a first sentence that is likely to grab the reader's attention *precisely* because it does not begin with a tired old phrase the reader has seen on the screen time and time again.

EXAMPLE

STEP #1 The purpose of this e-mail letter is

STEP #2 The purpose of this e-mail letter is to share my belief that the ad agency must be replaced. Our market share has dropped 29% over the past nine months, and the agency has offered no solutions. Let's discuss at next week's board meeting.

STEP #3 The ad agency must be replaced. Our market share has dropped 29% over the past nine months, and the agency has offered no solutions. Let's discuss at next week's board meeting.

P A R T

III

Keys to Effective E-Mail

KEYS TO EFFECTIVE E-MAIL

Writing electronic documents is no different from writing other business correspondence in many ways: It must be clear, concise and inoffensive to the reader. Despite the "instant" nature of e-mail, it is still necessary to go through a process to compose a document that keeps the reader's attention. Reading this chapter and completing its exercises will help you write e-mail which will get your message across—and keep your documents out of the reader's electronic trash can!

The Benefits of Short, Simple Sentences

- Short sentences are easier to write, read and understand. Long sentences, always difficult to read, are particularly hard to read on-screen.

- Long sentences test the writer's ability to use grammar and punctuation correctly. A hurried e-mail reader is more likely to delete a confusing, error-filled message than take time to correct the writer's mechanical errors and decipher the document's meaning.

- Long sentences tend to bury ideas. Remember the inverted pyramid. Put short sentences and paragraphs to work, communicating your primary message clearly, right from the beginning of the document.

- Limit most sentences to one major idea, and restrict most letters and memos to no more than three main points.

EDITING YOUR ON-SCREEN WRITING

The following long, heavily punctuated sentence challenges the recipient's ability to read and understand what the writer is saying. Could you blame the reader for deleting this message from the screen?

> I am writing this e-mail memo to confirm that the highway department will begin work on the repaving of Main Street the week of May 1, and we hope to complete the job within 30 days, but you need to be aware of the fact that weather conditions will impact our ability to start and finish on time, so if we experience a particularly rainy or cold spring, we may not be able to meet the June 1 deadline set forth by city council.

Begin your editing process by underlining the main point(s) and circling any unnecessary coordinating conjunctions (*and, or, nor, for, but, so, yet*), commas, and words. In our version, which follows, we have used bold to indicate unnecessary conjunctions and italics for unnecessary words:

> *I am writing this e-mail memo to confirm that* <u>the highway department will begin</u> *work on the* <u>repaving</u> *of* <u>Main Street the week of May 1,</u> **and** <u>we hope to complete the job within 30 days,</u> **but** *you need to be aware of the fact that* <u>weather conditions will impact our ability to</u> *start* **and** <u>finish on time,</u> so <u>if we experience a particularly rainy or cold spring, we may not be able to meet the June 1 deadline</u> *set forth by* <u>city council.</u>

Now rewrite the sentence, deleting unnecessary conjunctions, words and phrases. The result? A short, simple sentence.

> The highway department will begin repaving Main Street the week of May 1, completing the job by city council's June 1 deadline, barring weather delays.

Another option works equally well. Write two short sentences.

> The highway department will begin repaving Main Street the week of May 1. Unless the weather delays us, we will complete the job within the city council's 30-day deadline.

EXERCISE

The following sentences are too long. Underline the main point(s) of each sentence, circle any unnecessary conjunctions, and place brackets around needless words or phrases. Then rewrite as short, readable sentences.

1. The Yummy Pet Food Company is looking for 100 consumers to participate in an online survey of pet food buying habits, and we are willing to pay each participant $100 for his or her time and trouble, but we must begin our survey next Monday, so, if you are interested in participating, please e-mail us today, sending your e-mail to the attention of Miss Kitty Paas in the marketing department.

    _____

    _____

    _____

2. This e-mail message has been written to alert all my clients of my new e-mail address, which becomes effective January 1, and will make me available to respond to client needs more quickly, but if, in the interim, you need to reach me, please don't hesitate to contact me the good old-fashioned way, via voicemail.

    _____

    _____

    _____

3. Please do not use the company's e-mail system for personal purposes, such as advertising cars and other items for sale, or notifying coworkers of the birth or wedding of a child, and please remember that this e-mail system is monitored by management, and we will not tolerate the use of off-color language, offensive jokes or other inappropriate material, and if the personal and inappropriate use of the corporate e-mail does not come to an end, we will be forced to take disciplinary action against the violators, so knock it off.

    _____

    _____

    _____

POWER OR PASTE?

One of the most effective ways to develop a clean, clear writing style is to eliminate any surplus words from your sentences. There are two types of words in a writer's arsenal:

► **POWER** words convey the meaning of your sentences.

► **PASTE** words hold your sentences together as tight, grammatical units.

Your goal is to write sentences that contain more power than paste. The following pasty sentences create a weak paragraph:*

> This is a response I have written to one customer who recently shared his thoughts about his concerns for our return policy.
> I send it to you because I believe we need to develop and implement a more customer-oriented approach to service.

Let's analyze these sentences, underlining the power words and highlighting the paste words with italic type:

> *This is a response I have written to* <u>one customer</u> *who recently* <u>shared</u> *his thoughts about his* <u>concerns for our return policy.</u>
> *I send it to you because I believe* <u>we need to develop and implement a more customer-oriented approach to service.</u>

These two sentences together contain 21 power words and 22 paste words. That's too much paste. The writer's primary message, *the need to develop and implement a more customer-oriented approach to service,* comes at the end of the paragraph. In accordance with the inverted pyramid format, the writer's main message should lead the paragraph:

> We need to develop and implement more customer-oriented service. As one concerned customer recently said of our return policy . . .

---

* See the discussion of working words vs. glue words in the work of Richard C. Wydick, *Plain English for Lawyers,* 3rd ed. Durham, NC: Carolina Academic Press, 1994, pp. 7–10.

EXERCISE

For the following exercise, underline the power words, circle the paste, and tally each. Rewrite the sentences, eliminating as much paste as possible and making any changes necessary to strengthen each sentence.

1. In the event that the building loses power and the lights go off during working hours, all employees are instructed to remain seated at their desks and await the instructions of the department manager who is assigned to supervise the activity of the department.

   _____ *Number of Power Words*   _____ *Number of Paste Words*

   _____

   _____

   _____

2. I am sending this e-mail to all members of our association's board of directors to notify each and every member of the board of directors that effective the first of the new year the board will meet every third Monday of each month for the purpose of discussing association business matters.

   _____ *Number of Power Words*   _____ *Number of Paste Words*

   _____

   _____

   _____

3. Per your e-mail directive of April 1: My understanding is that there is to be no more parking of employee cars in parking spots designated for visitors to the company, nor is there to be any further tolerance of healthy company workers parking their vehicles in spaces that have been designated for disabled persons.

   _____ *Number of Power Words*   _____ *Number of Paste Words*

   _____

   _____

   _____

USING THE ACTIVE VOICE

As a general rule, business documents should be written in the active, not the passive, voice. Writing in the active voice will ensure that your electronic sentences are short, simple and easy to read.

Unsure what constitutes the active voice? Simply ask yourself *"Who is doing what to whom?"* Then write your sentence, focusing on the three w's: **who, what** and **whom**.

Consider the following passive sentence:

> It is possible for the accountants to conduct and complete an audit in 30 days.

ANALYSIS: The **accountants** are the **actors** [*who*].

Conduct and **complete** constitute the **action** [*what*].

An **audit** is the **object** [*whom*].

The following rewritten, active sentence eliminates all unnecessary words and focuses on actor, action and object:

> The accountants can complete an audit in 30 days.

Notice that the nine-word active sentence is much shorter than the lumbering 15-word passive sentence. Active constructions are always shorter than the passive. If you write in the active voice, your documents immediately will become tighter and more energetic.

EXERCISE

Rewrite these passive sentences, using the active voice and eliminating all unnecessary words. Your goal: breathe life into these weak constructions.

1. By now the memo should have been received by all intended recipients, and by the end of the week management should be receiving everyone's response via e-mail.

    _____

    _____

    _____

    _____

2. Employees who demonstrate adherence to company protocol and procedures shall be rewarded by management when it comes time for performance reviews.

    _____

    _____

    _____

    _____

3. Because the pilfering of office supplies by employees is a growing problem at headquarters, the director of human resources is looking for ways to screen job applicants' honesty.

    _____

    _____

    _____

    _____

SELECTING THE RIGHT TONE

Before starting to write, take a few minutes to think about the *five w's*:

► *Who are you writing to?* How much does the reader know about your subject? What prejudices does the reader have that could influence acceptance of your document? How does the reader feel about you? How experienced is your reader with e-mail? What will it take to convince the reader to act?

► *What is the primary purpose of your e-mail?* Are you trying to persuade readers to act, inform them of a problem or an event, elicit a response to a question? Do you have more than one purpose?

► *When and where does the action take place?* Does the reader need to be concerned about a deadline? What about logistics? Do you need to provide an address, a meeting time or directions? Before writing, gather every fact the reader needs in order to make a decision.

► *Why should the reader care about your e-mail message?* How interested in your topic is the reader? Will the reader benefit by acting on your document? Will there be negative fallout if the reader does not act? What information does the reader need in order to make a decision? Think about your message from the reader's point of view, and communicate benefits early in the document.

USING CONVERSATIONAL LANGUAGE

The most effective tone for business correspondence is a professional, yet conversational, tone. How to strike that tone? Imagine you are at a professional cocktail party, attended by colleagues, supervisors and customers. How would you speak? What type of language would you use? You would likely be conversational, yet professional, using language everyone would understand. When you write, use the same type of language and tone.

Bending a Few Rules to Strike an Appropriate Tone

► **CONTRACTIONS AREN'T BAD.**

Unless you are writing a particularly formal document, go ahead and use contractions. We use contractions when we speak in business settings, and there's nothing wrong with incorporating them into business writing.

► **FEEL FREE TO END A SENTENCE WITH A PREPOSITION.**

If you never ended a sentence with a preposition (*for, by, at, about, in, to, with, from,* etc.) your writing would be terribly stiff, boring and sometimes unreadable. *What is your e-mail message about?* makes considerably more sense than *About what is your e-mail message?*

► *I, WE* AND *YOU* **BELONG IN BUSINESS WRITING.**

The purpose of most e-mail is to persuade the reader to take some sort of action. Persuasion requires connection on a human level. It's hard to connect if you depersonalize your writing by eliminating all the pronouns.

► **AND ANOTHER THING.**

Go right ahead and start your sentence with a coordinating conjunction (*and, or, nor, for, but, so, yet*) to create a smooth transition from one sentence or thought to another.

USING CONVERSATIONAL LANGUAGE (continued)

Avoiding Conversational Pitfalls

▶ **HUMOR.** Unless you are a professional humorist, don't try to tell jokes or incorporate humor into your writing. E-mail is an impersonal medium that offers none of the benefits of inflection, facial expression or body language. If you must use humor, add a smiley mark or electronic shorthand (see Part IV) as a cue to help your reader understand your intent. But remember that not all e-mail users are familiar with these notations, so use them judiciously.

▶ **CLICHÉS.** In the world of business writing, clichés can take several forms.

- **Compound constructions:** *at that point in time* rather than *then; in the event that* versus *if; subsequent to* for *after*.

- **Redundant pairs:** *if and when; each and every; ready and willing*.

- **Redundant modifiers:** *official* e-mail from headquarters; *seriously* destroying our earth.

In addition to being trite and overused, clichés add unnecessary words. Do your reader and yourself a favor: eliminate clichés.

▶ **TECHNICAL LANGUAGE.** If you are sending a technical e-mail document to a reader or group of readers who share your expertise, it is probably all right to use technical language. But that does not free you to write dull, unreadable messages. Even with technical material, the basics hold: write in the active voice; eliminate unnecessary words; adhere to the mechanical rules of good writing; and write with your reader in mind.

Before you start writing in technical terms, think about hidden readers. Is there any possibility your e-mail will be read by a wider audience than you intend? If so, accommodate the nontechnical readers by including an executive summary at the beginning of your document.

► **ABBREVIATIONS.** Use legitimate abbreviations to shorten e-mail messages only if your readers—intended and hidden—will recognize and understand them. Don't overdo it. Too many abbreviations can make a sentence hard to read.

Example: I received your message an **hr.** ago and intend to act on it **ASAP.** I am curious, however. Did you **cc** the manager of the **E** Coast office as well?

Clarify an uncommon abbreviation on the first reference by writing it out and citing the abbreviation in parentheses. Then use the abbreviation throughout the rest of the document.

Example: The findings of the Electronic Messaging Association (EMA) indicate phenomenal growth for e-mail.

The trend is to omit periods within abbreviations. In general, place periods after abbreviations with all lowercase letters (*e.g., mfg.;*). Place no periods after abbreviations with all uppercase letters (*FYI; PS).* And be mindful of abbreviations that always require periods (*A.M.; P.M.; Mr.; Mrs.; Dr.).*

► **ACRONYMS.** Electronic acronyms have found their way into e-mail messages. If you have any doubt that your intended reader will understand an acronym, don't use it.

ACRONYMS AHEAD

Popular Electronic Acronyms

BCNU	be seeing you		**OBTW**	oh, by the way
BRB	be right back		**OIC**	oh, I see
BTW	by the way		**PLS**	please
CUL	see you later		**PMFJI**	pardon me for jumping in
F2F	face to face		**PRES**	presentation
FAQ	frequently asked question		**PTP**	pardon the pun
FOAF	friend of a friend		**QTY'S**	quantities
FWIW	for what it's worth		**REC'D**	received
FYA	for your amusement		**RGDS**	regards
FYEO	for your eyes only		**ROTF**	rolling on the floor
FYI	for your information		**ROTFL**	rolling on the floor laughing
GMTA	great minds think alike		**THX**	thanks
HHOK	ha-ha, only kidding		**TIA**	thanks in advance
IMHO	in my humble opinion		**TMRW**	tomorrow
IOW	in other words		**TTFN**	ta-ta for now
LOL	laughing out loud		**WB**	welcome back
MOTOS	member of the opposite sex		**WRT**	with regards to
MOTSS	member of the same sex		**WTG**	way to go
MSGS	messages		**YR**	your
NLT	no later than			

ELIMINATING SEXIST LANGUAGE

With increasing numbers of women in the workforce, it's important for e-mail writers to avoid sexist language that could offend clients, rankle colleagues or irritate hidden readers.

In the past, masculine pronouns (*he, him, his, himself*) were used to refer to both men and women. That practice is no longer acceptable. Now writers must look for more politically sensitive alternatives.

Short of adopting the cumbersome *he/she* or *he or she* construction, what's a gender-sensitive e-mail writer to do?

Strategies to Keep Your E-Mail Gender-Neutral

► **ELIMINATE THE OFFENDING PRONOUN**

Don't write: The busy executive should try to read the e-mail that is sent to **him** by clients and vendors daily.

Write: The busy executive should try to read the e-mail sent by clients and vendors daily.

► **REPEAT THE NOUN AND REWRITE**

Don't write: A toddler cannot understand why Mom would be frightened if she caught **him** with a match.

Write: A toddler cannot understand why Mom would be frightened if she caught **the toddler** with a match.

► **SWITCH TO A PLURAL ANTECEDENT NOUN WITH A PLURAL PRONOUN**

Don't write: An e-mail **writer** should make every effort to use correct grammar and punctuation in **his** writing.

Write: E-mail **writers** should make every effort to use correct grammar and punctuation in **their** writing.

ELIMINATING SEXIST LANGUAGE
(continued)

▶ **USE THE GENERIC PRONOUN** *ONE*

Don't write: A novice PC user is likely to find the local computer retailer and a reputable online bookseller **his** best sources of basic technical information.

Write: A novice PC user is likely to find the local computer retailer and a reputable online bookseller **one's** best sources of basic technical information.

▶ **REWRITE USING** *WHO*

Don't write: The assumption of many e-mail users is that if a writer makes an effort to correct **his** grammar and proofread **his** document, **he** is wasting time.

Write: The assumption of many e-mail users is that a writer **who** makes an effort to correct a document's grammar and proofread is wasting time.

▶ **USE AN ARTICLE (***A, AN, THE, THIS, THAT, THESE, THOSE***)**

Don't write: The contractor received a healthy bonus for **his** quick, professional work.

Write: The contractor received a healthy bonus for **the** quick, professional work.

▶ **WRITE IN THE IMPERATIVE MOOD—***GIVE A COMMAND*

Don't write: The e-mail writer must take the greatest care when **he** is using copywritten reference material.

Write: E-mail writers: Take the greatest care when using copywritten reference material.

► **REWORD THE SENTENCE**

Don't write: A writer who decides not to footnote source material puts **his** reputation at risk.

Write: Failure to footnote source material puts a writer's reputation at risk.

► **USE THEM, THEY OR THEIR . . .** *IF YOU DON'T MIND RANKLING A FEW READERS*

This option violates the long-standing rule of grammar that a singular noun takes a singular pronoun. Along with increased concern for political correctness, however, comes a growing acceptance of the use of the plural pronoun (*they, their, them*) with a singular antecedent noun.

While traditionalists discourage the practice, it is now acceptable to write, for example: *An e-mail user who receives a flame should give careful consideration to **their** attacker's motive.*

EXERCISE

Rewrite the following two sentences, eliminating masculine pronouns and creating gender-neutral constructions.

1. Any employee who does not understand the department's e-mail policy should schedule a meeting with his supervisor.

   _____

   _____

   _____

2. The instructor must take the greatest care when he is explaining new concepts to his students.

   _____

   _____

   _____

EXTINGUISHING FLAMES

An e-mail *flame* is a hostile message that is blunt, rude, insensitive or obscene. Sending this type of message is called *flaming.*

Flames ignite quickly, as people who are upset by something they have read online send back a quick, angry reply. One flame can start an online *flame war,* involving numerous people transmitting angry electronic messages back and forth. Flames are unique to e-mail, as the slow pace of traditional mail does not accommodate immediate, heated reaction. Before sending a flame, ask yourself the following questions:

- *Would I say this to a person's face?* If not, don't send the e-mail.

- *Would I be embarrassed if this message were read by my boss or a customer, colleague or other reader whose opinion matters to me?* If so, extinguish the flame.

- *Is it possible that the message I perceive to be a flame is actually an ill-phrased joke?* If you have any doubt, assume the best.

Controlling the Urge to Flame

▶ *Keep your emotions in check.* Even though it's possible to respond instantly to an offensive e-mail message, don't do it. Walk away from the flame, returning to the screen when you feel less heated.

▶ *Never use obscene or abusive language in e-mail messages.*

▶ *Write your response thoughtfully and proofread carefully before sending it.* The more distance you can put between a flame and your response, the less likely you'll flame back.

▶ *Avoid flaming in public forums.* If you want to respond to a message, do so directly. Don't risk drawing others into a flame war.

PART

IV

Polishing Your Cybergrammar Skills

ELIMINATING MECHANICAL ERRORS

In the battle for the reader's on-screen attention, carefully written e-mail that is free from mechanical errors is sure to win. A few rules and some practical advice can help you reduce errors and enhance effectiveness.

► **BEWARE THE EXCLAMATION POINT.**

Many e-mail writers mistakenly believe they can inject life into their electronic writing—and elicit reader interest—by slapping an exclamation point onto the end of every important sentence. Don't fall into this trap!!! Put power in your writing with descriptive language and well-crafted sentences. Use exclamation points sparingly, if at all.

► **PLAY THE NUMBERS GAME ACCURATELY.**

• Write out numbers between one and nine. From 10 on, use Arabic numerals.

• Never start a sentence with a number; write the word out.

• When writing about money, use Arabic numbers unless you are expressing large, rounded-off sums or are talking about money in general terms.

   EXAMPLE: The company's net profit this year was $12 million (rounded off), versus a few million (general terms) the year before.

► **QUOTE CORRECTLY.**

• Periods and commas always go inside the closing quotation mark. No exceptions.

   EXAMPLE: I read a review in which the critic called our chef "the master of the marinade."

• Semicolons and colons always go outside the closing quotation mark. No exceptions.

   EXAMPLE: I read a review in which the critic called our chef "the master of the marinade"; I agree wholeheartedly.

ELIMINATING MECHANICAL ERRORS (continued)

► **INTRODUCE QUOTATIONS IN ONE OF FOUR WAYS:**

1. With no punctuation before the quote.

   EXAMPLE: At the deposition, the executive maintained *"I never used the company's e-mail for personal use."*

2. With a comma before the quote.

   EXAMPLE: At the deposition, the executive maintained, *"I never used the company's e-mail for personal use."*

3. With a colon before the quote.

   EXAMPLE: At the deposition, the executive maintained: *"I never used the company's e-mail for personal use."*

4. With a period followed by the quote standing alone as an independent sentence.

   EXAMPLE: At the deposition, the executive maintained her position. *"I never used the company's e-mail for personal use."*

Any of the four methods is correct; the choice is a matter of style.

► **ADD SOME DASH TO YOUR WRITING.**

The dash is a handy, versatile punctuation mark that can add emphasis to incidental comments. Used in place of a comma or parentheses, a dash can be produced on the keyboard with two unspaced hyphens with no space before or after.

EXAMPLE: The intern forgot--if he ever knew--the correct way to address an e-mail message to the Dublin, Ireland office.

Reviewing Punctuation Basics

When it comes to punctuation, many business writers have trouble remembering what punctuation mark goes where, when. Taking time to debate the placement of a comma or the correct use of a semicolon defeats e-mail's purpose as a speedy communications vehicle. If you feel unclear about the mechanics of writing, this refresher should help.

USING COMMAS CORRECTLY

Correct comma usage is often a matter of good judgment. If you are unsure of when to use a comma, the following rules should help.

► At the end of a complete, grammatical sentence, use a comma if the next grammatical sentence begins with a coordinating conjunction (*and, or, nor, for, but, so, yet*).

   EXAMPLE: My staff's performance has always exceeded expectations, and I see no reason for that to change.

► When two clauses share a subject, omit the comma if the subject is not expressed in the second clause.

   EXAMPLE: An effective e-mail document should be brief and should be readable.

   Add the comma only if the subject is expressed on both sides of the coordinating conjunction.

   EXAMPLE: An effective e-mail document should be brief, and it should be readable.

► Serial commas separate two or more items in a list. You have a choice of two constructions. One, you can place a comma after each item in the list: *Please respond via e-mail, voicemail, or snail mail.* Or two, you can omit the comma before the final item in the list: *Please respond via e-mail, voicemail or snail mail.* Whichever option you choose, be sure to maintain consistency of construction throughout your document.

► Always put the final comma in a list of two or more if its absence would lead to ambiguity:

   EXAMPLE A: The bride asked to see rings featuring rubies, emeralds, sapphires, and diamonds.

   EXAMPLE B: The bride asked to see rings featuring rubies, emeralds, sapphires and diamonds.

   ANALYSIS: The comma is essential to understanding how many rings the bride wants to see. In Example A, we assume the bride wants to see four types of rings. The conclusion drawn from Example B is that she wants to see only three types.

   When in doubt about placing a comma between paired adjectives, silently insert *and* between the adjectives. If the *and* makes sense (*a compelling and timely memo*), place a comma between the adjectives (*a compelling, timely memo*). If the *and* seems awkward (*a happy and little girl*), omit the comma (*a happy little girl*).

USING COMMAS CORRECTLY (continued)

*Six Almost Absolute Comma Rules**

1. Never put a comma after an introductory subordinating conjunction such as *because, if, although, while, since, as, before* or *after.*

NOT THIS: Because, e-mail is a growing communications vehicle, more people are buying personal computers.

2. Resist a comma after the introductory coordinating conjunctions *and, or, nor, for, but, so, yet.*

NOT THIS: But, we cannot assume that all PC owners are adept at e-mail. And, we must be patient with colleagues who are e-mail novices.

3. Writers who punctuate heavily may put a comma after *and, or, nor, for, but, so, yet* if an introductory word or phrase follows: *Yet, as electronic communication becomes more prevalent, even the most reluctant computer user will warm up to e-mail.* This convention is a matter of taste.

4. Generally, put a comma after introductory words or phrases—*however, nevertheless, regardless, instead, on the other hand, as a result, consequently, moreover, furthermore, that is, also, fortunately, obviously, allegedly, incidentally*—that comment on the whole of the following sentence.

EXAMPLE: Furthermore, research indicates that electronic writing can be just as powerful as traditional writing.

5. Always separate an introductory word, phrase or clause—no matter how short—from what follows if the reader might misunderstand.

EXAMPLE: When the writer composes a compelling e-mail lead the reader has no trouble reading or understanding the document. (A comma between *lead* and *the* would help the reader grasp the meaning of this sentence.)

6. If you open a sentence with a short introductory phrase before a short subject, you don't need a comma:

EXAMPLE: Once again we find ourselves turning to a new and exciting means of communication. (No need to follow *Once again* with a comma.)

---

* For the concept of the *Almost Absolute Rules,* we are indebted to Joseph M. Williams, *Style: Ten Lessons in Clarity & Grace.* Glenview, IL: Scott, Foresman and Company, 1981, pp. 189–91.

MORE PUNCTUATION TIPS

Using the Semicolon

At the end of a grammatical sentence, use a semicolon if the next grammatical sentence does not begin with a coordinating conjunction (*and, or, nor, for, but, so, yet*).

> **EXAMPLE:** *E-mail is a revolutionary communication tool; within the decade most business and personal correspondence will be delivered electronically.*

You can also use a semicolon to join statements too closely related to be split into two sentences by a period but not related closely enough for a comma to suffice.

> **EXAMPLE:** *My printer is jamming up; I'll have to take it in for repair.*

Using the Colon

► Capitalize after the colon when the material following it consists of one or more independent clauses.

> **EXAMPLE:** *We like our new e-mail software for two reasons: It is readily accessible. In addition, it offers a variety of type and color options.*

► Capitalize after the colon if the material that follows it appears on a new line.

> **EXAMPLE:** *We are looking for recruits with three traits:*
> - *A willingness to relocate*
> - *An advanced degree*
> - *An understanding of our industry*

► Capitalize after the colon if what follows is the first word of a quotation.

> **EXAMPLE:** *Tom's response to his neighbor's complaint was short and to the point: "Believe me, my son is not guilty of picking flowers from your garden."*

► Do not capitalize after the colon when the material following it cannot stand alone as a sentence.

> **EXAMPLE:** *Association members were asked to bring three items to the training session: pens, paper and enthusiasm.*

MORE PUNCTUATION TIPS (continued)

Saving Space with Ellipses

► Use ellipses (three spaced periods) to omit words or sentences from a direct quotation.

EXAMPLE: *The CEO announced last week that "Our shareholders and employees . . . deserve a vote of thanks for sticking with us through trying times."*

► Add a fourth ellipsis period to mark the end of a sentence.

EXAMPLE: *The CEO thrilled the investors with his comments: "E-mail usage is growing rapidly . . . . The Electronic Messaging Association reports e-mail transmissions in the workplace will total about 1.2 trillion in the year 2000, up 6.5 times over the 1994 level of 184 billion."*

► Adding the fourth ellipsis period and capitalizing *"The"* signals the reader that the end of the first sentence has been omitted, and that possibly several sentences or paragraphs have been removed before starting the next sentence. Grammarians generally agree that ellipses should be used to indicate omissions *within* quotations, not at their beginning or end. Most readers will assume a quote has been pulled from a larger context.

SPELLING COUNTS!

Think no one pays attention to electronic spelling? For some reason, even the busiest reader will zero right in on a misspelling. Don't give readers any excuse to delete your document from the screen. Spelling errors and typos undermine your credibility and your e-mail's impact. Proofreading on screen is a tough but indispensable part of the electronic writing process.

Five Electronic Spelling Tips

1. **Use your spell-checker program if your e-mail package is equipped with one.** Remember, however, that the electronic spell checker cannot correct usage. For example, it can't distinguish between *to, two,* and *too; affect* and *effect;* or *its* and *it's.* Proofread manually first, using the electronic system for your final check.

2. **Purchase and use a good, up-to-date dictionary.** In addition to giving correct spellings, the dictionary is a good reference tool for proper usage and a valuable source of synonyms.

3. **Do not stop writing to look up or spell check every word that looks funny to you.** Wait until your document is completely written, then go back to the beginning and proofread thoroughly.

4. **Take your time with important documents.** Once you push *Send,* your e-mail message is on its way and probably cannot be retrieved. Never put in writing—electronic or traditional—anything that could come back to haunt you. If your document is particularly important or sensitive, you owe it to yourself to slow down and conduct a careful review of spelling, content and mechanics. If time allows, print and proofread a hard copy before sending your document into cyberspace. When in doubt about the appropriateness of your message, impose a 48-hour cooling-off period before sending it. If time is short, ask a trusted colleague to proofread your message before you send it.

5. **Invest in a writing manual that covers the most commonly misspelled words and typical grammatical goofs.** Check with an online bookseller to see what is currently available.

SPELLING COUNTS! (continued)

Writers often confuse a number of "word pairs" that either sound alike or have similar meanings. The rule to follow is simple: If you have any doubt about the way in which you are using a word, look it up in the dictionary. Following is a sampling of words most often confused and misused by business writers:

Commonly Misspelled Words

► AFFECT/EFFECT:

Affect *(the verb)* means to influence. *EXAMPLE: The spelling errors* ***affected*** *the reader's impression of the writer.*

Effect *(the noun)* means to produce a result. *EXAMPLE: The* ***effect*** *of the spelling errors was a loss of credibility.*

► AS/LIKE:

As is used as a conjunction and is followed by a group of words including a subject and verb. *EXAMPLE: Yesterday's e-mail messages from headquarters were confusing,* ***as*** *they always are when the writer incorporates too much jargon.*

Like is used as a preposition. *EXAMPLE: The college intern could attach e-mail documents* ***like*** *a Cyberspace veteran.*

► COMPRISED OF/COMPOSED OF

The whole **comprises** the parts; the parts **compose** the whole. *EXAMPLE: The alphabet* ***comprises*** *26 letters. Twenty-six letters* ***compose*** *the alphabet.*

► ITS/IT'S

Its is a possessive, requiring no apostrophe. **It's** is a contraction, meaning *it is. EXAMPLE:* **It's** *a well-written e-mail message that persuades* **its** *intended reader to act.*

► LAY/LIE

Lay means to put something down and takes an object. *EXAMPLE:* ***Lay*** *your PC on the table.*

Lie means to recline and does not take an object. *EXAMPLE: You can't* ***lie*** *on this mattress.* Among the most commonly confused words in the English language, **lay** and **lie** cause particular grief in the past tense, where **lay** becomes **laid** and **lie** becomes **lay.** *EXAMPLE: After she* ***laid*** *her PC down, it continued to* ***lay*** *there for days.*

PUNCTUATING WITH SMILEYS AND SHORTHAND

Unlike one-on-one meetings and telephone conversations, e-mail is a communications vehicle devoid of inflection, facial expression and body language. To help readers interpret the e-mail writer's attitude and tone, *smileys*—also known as *emoticons*—were created as visual shorthand. Smileys, which are created with standard keyboard characters, are used by some writers to substitute for facial expressions and body language. Generally the smiley follows the punctuation mark at the end of a sentence.

The equivalent of e-mail slang, smileys should be used sparingly, and not at all in business writing. Those unfamiliar with smileys will not understand them; more experienced readers will label you an e-mail novice if you overuse them. Rely on the strength of your writing—not smileys, exclamation points or other gimmicks—to communicate your intended message in the appropriate tone.

PUNCTUATING WITH SMILEYS AND SHORTHAND (continued)

Popular Smileys

SMILEY-EMOTICON	DESCRIPTION	SMILEY-EMOTICON	DESCRIPTION
:-)	happy; kidding; smiling; grinning	>:P	sticking tongue out
:-[	sad sarcasm	:-P	sticking tongue out
:-(	sad; angry; chagrined	8-)	wide-eyed
;-(	feel like crying	8-O	shocked; amazed
:-&	tongue-tied	:-|	apathetic
:!-(	crying	:-/	skeptical; perplexed; resigned
:-<	very upset	:-o	shocked or amazed
%-)	happy confused; eyes crossed; smirking	:->	sarcastic smile
:-||	angry	:-]	happy sarcasm or smirk
%-(	sad confused	;^)	smirking smile
:-(o)	yelling	(:/)	sarcasm
:-*	kiss	<:/&	stomach in knots
:-D	laughing; demonic laugh	>:-)	devilish
:-\	undecided	O:-)	angelic
;-)	winking	X-(	brain dead
:-#	my lips are sealed		

Some e-mail writers find smileys limiting, and use electronic shorthand or a combination of smileys and acronyms to express emotions.

SHORTHAND	EMOTION
<g>	grin
<grin>	grin
<s>	sigh
<gasp>	gasp
<l>	laugh
<laughing out loud>	laughing out loud
<lol>	laughing out loud
<jk>	just kidding
<>	no comment

Again, don't use electronic shorthand if you have any question about your reader's ability to understand it.

P A R T

V

Formatting Your E-Mail Document

FORMATTING YOUR DOCUMENT

Readability is the name of the game when it comes to formatting your document. If it isn't legible, the recipients may not have the patience to wade through your message, no matter how important. Here are some guidelines for making your documents easy to read.

Choosing the Right Typeface

Few things are harder to read than e-mail composed with unusual type or exceptionally large or small characters. If your subject is business-related, create a polished, professional look by using a standard typeface such as Times New Roman, Courier or Arial. And stick with the 10-point to 12-point font sizes most readers are comfortable with:

10-point Times New Roman

11-point Courier

12-point Arial

For headings or other special elements within your e-mail, a larger font size produces a nice effect, but should be used sparingly.

If your topic is personal, you can inject personality into your writing by using a typeface such as Bellevue, Hobo or Goudy Handtooled to communicate the casual tone of your message:

10-point Bellevue

11-point Hobo

12-point Goudy Handtooled

A good typeface policy for all e-mail: not too small; not too large; not too ornate.

RESISTING THE URGE TO USE CAPITAL OR LOWERCASE LETTERS

In an effort to draw attention to on-screen messages, many e-mail writers use all capital letters. Bad idea. A message written in all uppercase letters is more difficult to read than one written in standard style. The human eye is used to reading a mixture of uppercase and lowercase letters. When you draft e-mail in all uppercase letters, you run the risk of slowing down—and annoying—a reader unaccustomed to this type of visual presentation.

By the same token, resist the urge to write e-mail messages in the lowercase. It may be quicker to write in all caps or all lowercase, but the result will be more difficult to read.

A Readability Quiz

Test your reaction to the following passage, written in three styles: all capitals; all lowercase letters; and the standard mixture of uppercase and lowercase. Which do you find most readable?

1. EMPLOYEE USE OF E-MAIL CAN EXPOSE A BUSINESS TO LIABILITY BASED ON A MESSAGE'S CONTENT. IN 1995 CHEVRON PAID $2.2 MILLION TO FOUR FEMALE EMPLOYEES TO SETTLE A SEXUAL HARASSMENT LAWSUIT AFTER THE EMPLOYEES CLAIMED THEY WERE HARASSED BY E-MAIL.*

2. employee use of e-mail can expose a business to liability based on a message's content. in 1995 chevron paid $2.2 million to four female employees to settle a sexual harassment lawsuit after the employees claimed they were harassed by e-mail.

3. Employee use of e-mail can expose a business to liability based on a message's content. In 1995 Chevron paid $2.2 million to four female employees to settle a sexual harassment lawsuit after the employees claimed they were harassed by e-mail.

---

* Philip Lilly, "Vipers in E-Mail's Garden," *Business First,* of Columbus, Ohio, *Tech Now: A User's Guide to the Internet* Supplement, 1 November 1996, p. 18A.

CREATING EMPHASIS WITH BULLETS AND NUMBERS

Emphasize important copy points by creating lists with bullets or numbers. Because there is no standard bullet character on the keyboard, you may want to substitute an asterisk (*) or dash (—). Remember:

* Be consistent. If your list starts with an asterisk, it should end with one.

* Write complete sentences or sentence fragments, but be consistent.

* Begin each bullet point with a capital letter.

Numbered lists create the greatest emphasis:

1. Keep each line short.

2. Indent your list to maximize impact.

3. Add emphasis by double-spacing and leaving plenty of white space.

Don't be afraid of white space. An extra line or two before and after an important section—in a list or within a paragraph—adds impact and enhances readability.

As an alternative to numbered lists, you can construct lists within paragraphs. This approach saves space while maximizing readability.

EXAMPLE: *Numbered lists are most effective when the writer adheres to three rules: (1) Keep lists short; (2) Indent lists for maximum readability; and (3) Create white space by double-spacing.*

Selecting an Appropriate Screen Color

Your e-mail package may give you the option of changing the background or foreground colors of your message. Don't feel obligated to exercise this option. While a purple background with green letters might create an interesting look, it also may undercut your credibility. For business correspondence, use a neutral or light background with dark letters in the foreground. Unusual screen colors can be hard to read, and they can detract from or conflict with the tone of your communication.

ACKNOWLEDGING SOFTWARE LIMITATIONS

Your ability to send e-mail messages that incorporate interesting type and colors is only as good as your reader's e-mail software. Before adding attention-getting typefaces, color, margins, italics, underlining, or other graphic devices, make sure your reader is able to receive your message as you create it. If your reader's e-mail software is incompatible with yours, the results can be disastrous.

NOTE: If you are unsure of the capabilities of your recipient's software, it's advisable to restrict yourself to no more than 65 to 75 characters per line, pressing *Enter* or *Return* after each line. Doing so will ensure that each line is presentable, even if the recipient's software doesn't *word wrap,* or automatically stay within defined margins.

EMPHASIZING ELECTRONIC TEXT

Because of incompatibility problems among e-mail software packages, many electronic writers have adopted common conventions for italicizing and underlining text. Use these electronic symbols judiciously, however, as confusion may result if your reader is unfamiliar with them.

TO ITALICIZE: Insert an asterisk (*) on either side of the word or phrase to be italicized. For example, to italicize the word *authored*, surround it with asterisks: *The movie star *authored* her autobiography with help from an experienced ghostwriter.*

TO UNDERLINE: Add the underscore character before and after the copy to be underlined. For example, to underline *The American Heritage Dictionary,* introduce and follow it with the underscore character: *Every e-mail writer should own a good, up-to-date dictionary such as _The American Heritage Dictionary_.*

Maintaining Appropriate Margins

It is not unusual for people to receive dozens of e-mail messages daily. With that kind of volume, you need to do everything in your power to make your message stand out. One of the easiest ways to accomplish this is with margin settings. The following exercise highlights how attention to even the simplest details will result in eye-catching messages:

Set your left margin at 0 and your right margin at 100. Now type a message several sentences long. Notice how the text on the left is difficult to read, and the text on the right is invisible without using the scroll bar?

Now try setting your margins at 5 on the left and 75 on the right. Retype the paragraph. Isn't that better? Your entire message is now directly in front of you on the screen, easily accessible to even the busiest reader.

VI

Managing and Organizing Your E-Mail

MANAGING AND ORGANIZING YOUR E-MAIL

As e-mail becomes more prevalent, your inbox and outbox will begin to swell. Unless you know how to organize your electronic desktop, it will become difficult to find documents you have written or received when you need them. Here are some hints for keeping your documents handy, as well as tips on attaching files to your e-mail, and some electronic pitfalls to avoid.

Attaching Documents to Messages

Most e-mail messages will be contained on one screen, and only a small portion of the screen at that. On occasion, however, you may write an e-mail message that is so long the reader must scroll through the screen in order to read it all. That's not necessarily bad. Some topics warrant a little extra space. However, when you think your e-mail message has gone on too long, or you need to incorporate letterhead, charts or graphics into your message, it is time to attach a separate document. The attachment feature, available on most e-mail software, enables you to add, or attach, documents that have been created in separate files. Attachment software expands the capabilities of e-mail, allowing the writer to deliver longer, more comprehensive documents, including word processing, spreadsheets, charts and graphics.

MANAGING AND ORGANIZING YOUR E-MAIL (continued)

Before attaching a document, however, take a moment to consider its appropriateness.

▶ **Can Your Reader's E-Mail System Accommodate Your Attachment?**

There's no point sending an attachment if your reader can't open it. Before attaching a document to your e-mail message, consider the software your reader is using. When in doubt, send a quick e-mail or give your recipient a call. A little effort on the prewriting end will ultimately save time and eliminate frustration later.

▶ **Use the Attachment As Intended.**

In your e-mail message, provide a brief description of the attachment. But resist the temptation to go into detail. That's the attachment's job.

▶ **Generate Reader Interest in the Attachment.**

Use that brief description to sell your reader on the attachment's merits. Explain in a sentence or two what the attachment is and why the reader should take time to read it.

▶ **Don't Send an Attachment When a Brief Message Will Do.**

Before attaching a document, ask if it is really necessary. If a brief e-mail message will do the job, don't bother attaching a file.

▶ **Compress Extremely Large Files.**

Attaching extremely large documents—databases, graphics, spreadsheets—can be a problem. The time and resources needed to transmit exceptionally large documents can irritate local network administrators and Internet service providers. As an alternative, consider using a compression program to reduce the size of large attachments. Before compressing, however, make sure your recipient has the capability to decompress the file.

Attaching Files Step-By-Step

While e-mail packages vary, attaching files generally is a four-step process:

STEP #1 Select the attachment option on your screen. It may appear as the word *Attach* or as an icon symbolizing an attachment. Check your software manual if you are unclear about your system's icon.

STEP #2 Select the document to be attached from the appropriate folder.

STEP #3 Repeat the process if you are attaching multiple documents.

STEP #4 After you confirm your selection, your original e-mail message will reappear along with a list of attached document(s).

For specific instructions on how to attach documents to your e-mail, refer to the user's manual you received with your e-mail software.

NOTE: One very common attachment error is to send someone a message saying you are attaching a file, and then to send the e-mail without ever attaching it. This often happens when you get sidetracked with your message. You can avoid this problem by attaching your file before you compose your message.

AVOIDING INBOX CLUTTER

E-mail messages will pile up in your electronic inbox unless you take steps to manage them. Your electronic inbox is the appropriate place to keep current or relatively new messages requiring immediate attention. But once the immediacy of a message passes, either delete, print or save it.

Deleting is the quickest, easiest way to unclutter your e-mail inbox. Unless your organization's e-mail policy requires it, you probably don't need or want to keep every message you receive. If a message is unimportant, requires no action or reply, or is a junk posting, delete it.

Printing a hard copy of your electronic message may be appropriate, however, under the following circumstances:

- You think you will need the document later when you don't have access to your PC.

- Your organization demands you keep hard copies of all customer or vendor correspondence.

- You want to share an e-mail message with someone who is not online.

Filing and Archiving Saved E-Mail

To save e-mail messages on your computer without cluttering your inbox, file or archive them.

Filing is the organizing of active messages that you want to save on your computer for convenient access.

Archiving is the storing of older messages that no longer belong on your computer but don't necessitate deletion.

Filing e-mail is as simple as creating and labeling document folders to store individual messages. Depending on your e-mail package, you will probably take the following steps when filing:

1. Select the document you wish to file.

2. Select the folder in which you want to keep the document.

3. Give your document a file name.

4. Click on *Save.*

It is a good idea to conduct an annual review of all the documents in your folders. Archive those documents that you no longer need on your computer, but aren't ready to delete.

To archive a document, save the folders/documents to diskette, then delete the files from your computer. Using file compression software will make the files easier to manage. Store the archive diskettes in a safe place, off-site if they are particularly valuable.

> **Don't forget to back up your document folders regularly. All the organization in the world won't matter if you can't recover data in an emergency.**

BATTLING ELECTRONIC VIRUSES

Anytime you send or receive e-mail, you risk catching and spreading a computer virus. Some viruses are merely irritating, not destructive. You'll know you've been attacked by an annoying, nondestructive virus if, for example, you suddenly see little green men dancing across your screen, flashing distracting messages. Other viruses, sent with malicious intent, are more deadly. A destructive virus can erase files from your disk, impede system processing, and transfer itself from one computer to another.

E-mail attachments are the most common form of virus transportation. If you open an infected word-processing document, spreadsheet or other attachment, there's a good chance of catching the bug.

The best medicine is preventive: Never open an attachment unless you know the sender. Of course, sometimes your sender may not know a file is infected. Your best means of protection is to purchase virus detection software if your e-mail package is not equipped with this feature. Virus protection programs allow users to check e-mail transmissions for viruses before opening attachments.

ON A DIET? AVOID SPAM.

As an e-mail user, you will likely receive plenty of electronic junk mail, or *spam.* Junk e-mail primarily includes advertisements, get-rich-quick schemes and adult-oriented material. Electronic junk mailers typically gain access to e-mail addresses in four ways:

1. When you send e-mail that contains your return address, you run the risk of your recipient forwarding your address to someone else. Some companies exist solely to buy and sell electronic mailing lists.

2. Online service providers sometimes sell subscribers' addresses.

3. If you give your address to anyone over the Internet, you become vulnerable. Your e-mail address could be used by that site or sold to others.

4. Addresses can be intercepted as messages are transmitted through cyberspace. However, bad guys with that much technical expertise are probably looking for more valuable information, such as credit card numbers.

A Few Spam-Busting Techniques

► Delete unsolicited messages. A simple solution, deleting junk e-mail gives you a feeling of control over the situation.

► When sending e-mail messages to recipients you don't know, ask that your address not be forwarded or sold.

► Buy software to filter out unwanted messages. Some filtering programs are based on key words and phrases. Add *"get rich quick"* to your filter list, and messages containing that phrase will be deleted. Other filtering programs send unwanted messages to a dedicated folder, which you periodically delete without reading. The downside to this approach is that legitimate messages could slip through and be deleted along with the junk.

► For confidential messages, use encryption software that scrambles contents, making messages indecipherable to all but the intended recipient.

► Search the Internet for helpful information about electronic junk mail, cyberfraud and privacy laws.

► When you receive electronic junk mail, don't bother asking to be removed from the sender's list. The spammer probably won't comply.

A GLOSSARY OF WRITING AND E-MAIL TERMS

Acronym
A word formed from the first letters of a phrase's words. *Example: LOL for laughing out loud.*

Active Verb
A verb that expresses an action. *Examples: write, edit* and *type.*

Active Voice
The most powerful way to write. In the active voice, the subject (*the actor*) of the verb (*the action*) is also the subject of the sentence.

Address
The destination of an e-mail message.

Address Book
A collection of e-mail addresses.

Adjective
A part of speech that describes a noun. *Example: Paul owns a black (adjective) bicycle (noun).*

Adverb
A part of speech that modifies a verb, an adjective or another adverb. *Example: Paul happily (adverb) rides (verb) his black bike.*

Antecedent Noun
The noun for which a pronoun is substituted. *Example: Tim (antecedent noun) is enjoying his (pronoun) time on campus.*

Archiving
Storing old e-mail messages that warrant neither attention nor deletion.

Article
The words *a, an, the, this, that, these, those.*

Attachment
A computer file sent with an e-mail message. *Examples:* word processing documents, spreadsheets, databases or graphics.

Backup
Saving data to an external source such as a diskette or tape.

Bcc
Blind carbon copy

Cc
Carbon copy

CD-ROM	Acronym for *compact disk read-only memory*. Used for data storage.
Clause	A group of related words that include a verb and its subject. May be independent (a complete sentence) or dependent (an incomplete sentence).
Cliché	An overused word or phrase that has become part of everyday language.
Colon	A punctuation mark (:) that creates a pause, signaling readers to look ahead. Introduces a quotation, explanation or series of items.
Comma	A punctuation mark (,) that indicates a pause and separates ideas or elements in a sentence.
Compound Sentence	A sentence with at least two independent clauses, usually connected by a coordinating conjunction. *Example: Sammi is a collector of antiques, but she does not entirely dislike modern furniture.*
Compression	File management technique that shrinks data for easy transportation and storage.
Contraction	A word formed by combining two words and replacing one or more letters with an apostrophe. *Example: It's for it is.*
Coordinating Conjunction	A part of speech (*and, or, nor, for, but, so, yet*) that connects words and groups of words of the same rank: nouns with nouns, verbs with verbs, independent clauses with independent clauses, etc.
CPU	Acronym for *central processing unit*. The brains of the computer.
Cyberfraud	An illegal computer scam or con game.
Cybergrammar	The correct use of mechanics—*grammar, punctuation and spelling*—in e-mail documents.

A GLOSSARY OF WRITING AND E-MAIL TERMS (continued)

Cyberspace	The electronic environment in which people interact via computers.
Dash	A punctuation mark (—) that produces a sharp break between elements in a sentence.
Disk/Floppy Disk	A plastic or metallic object used to store computer data.
E-Mail	An electronic message transmitted between computers.
Electronic Correspondence	E-mail messages and attachments.
Electronic Jargon	Acronyms, abbreviations and slang used and understood by a limited number of e-mail users.
Electronic Shorthand	A means for e-mail writers to express emotion. Not understood by all e-mail users. ***Example:*** *<g> for grin.*
Emoticons	Electronic symbols of emotion. Also called *smileys.*
Encryption	The process of scrambling an e-mail message to ensure privacy. Once received, the message must be decoded by the recipient.
Executive Summary	Short section of copy preceding a lengthy or technical document. Highlights key points in conversational language.
Filing	The organization of active messages and/or files.
Filters	An e-mail program feature that allows the user to sort incoming messages.
Five Ws	*Who, what, when, where* and *why?* Five questions to ask before starting to write.
Flame	An angry or insulting e-mail message.

Folder	Related computer messages and/or documents that are stored together.
Forward	Retransmitting one e-mail message to a second user.
Gender	The grammatical categories of masculine, feminine or neuter.
Gender-Neutral Language	Words that indicate no bias, male or female.
Group List	A roster of e-mail addresses.
Hardware	Physical computer system components.
Hidden Reader	An unintended e-mail reader, unknown to the writer.
Icon	A symbol on the computer screen that depicts an action or function. For example, a paper-clip icon could signify the attachment feature.
Imperative Mood	Expresses a command. ***Example:*** *Writers: proofread carefully before distributing e-mail.*
Inbox	The place where received e-mail messages are stored.
Independent Clause	Has a subject and verb and can stand alone as a sentence.
Internet	A worldwide collection of computer networks. Home to the World Wide Web. Always capitalized. Synonymous with the *Net*.
Intended Reader	The person(s) to whom the e-mail writer addresses and sends a message.
Introductory Subordinating Conjunction	*Because, if, when, since, although*—words that serve as links.

A GLOSSARY OF WRITING AND E-MAIL TERMS (continued)

Inverted Pyramid The writing approach favored by journalists. The most important information or conclusion comes first, followed by information in descending order of importance.

Jargon Technical language or slang, unfamiliar to general readers.

Lead The first sentence(s) of the first paragraph.

Message A single e-mail communication. Generally limited to one page.

Modem Hardware device connecting a computer and phone line.

Net Synonymous with the *Internet.* A worldwide network of computers communicating in a common language via telephone lines or microwave links. Home of the World Wide Web.

Network Administrator Person responsible for operating and maintaining a computer network.

Noun Expresses the name of a person, place thing or idea.

Object Receives the action of a verb or comes at the end of a prepositional phrase. *Example: Carl chased (verb) the laughing toddler (object).*

Passive Voice The subject of the verb is the receiver, not the doer of the action. *Example: The offensive e-mail message (object) was sent (verb) by the disgruntled employee (subject as passive receiver).*

Period A punctuation mark (.) that signals the end of a sentence.

Possessive Case Indicates ownership. *Example: It's a well-written e-mail message that motivates its (possessive) reader to act.*

Priority	Designates an e-mail message's importance—*high, normal or low priority.* Lets readers know how quickly to open and act on a message.
Pronoun	A noun substitute: *I, me, you, he, she, it, they, etc.*
Quotation Marks	Punctuation marks ("*I*") that indicate the writer is repeating another writer's work word-for-word.
Recipient	The receiver, or reader, of an e-mail message.
Redundant Modifier	A word that means the same thing as the word it modifies. Examples: *completely dead, free gift, totally full.*
Redundant Pairs	Words that are commonly paired for no good reason. ***Examples:*** *each and every, any and all, willing and able.*
Relative Pronouns	The words *who, which* and *that.*
Reply	The response to an e-mail message.
Semicolon	A punctuation mark (;) used to separate independent clauses in a compound sentence. ***Example:*** *E-mail is a quick communications vehicle; everyone should try it.*
Sentence	A group of words that can stand alone as a complete thought.
Sexist Language	Indicates a male or female bias.
Signature	A personal identifier at the end of an e-mail message. May include the writer's name, company name and e-mail address.
Signature File	A predefined signature that can be inserted at the end of an e-mail message.
Smileys	Electronic symbols of emotion. Also called *emoticons.*

A GLOSSARY OF WRITING AND E-MAIL TERMS (continued)

Snail Mail　　　　　Traditional method of mailing letters via the post office.

Software　　　　　Computer programs such as e-mail or word processing.

Spam　　　　　Unsolicited junk mail delivered via e-mail.

Subject　　　　　The word that represents the person, place, thing, or idea the sentence is about.

Subject Line　　　　　Topic of an e-mail message.

Synonym　　　　　A word that is so close in meaning to another word it can be used in its place. ***Example:*** *speedy* for *quick*.

Traditional Correspondence　　　　　Nonelectronic writing.

Verb　　　　　The part of speech that expresses action.

Virus　　　　　An infectious computer bug. Symptoms range from mild distractions to major problems.

Word Wrap　　　　　Software feature that allows text to stay within defined margins. Eliminates the need to press *Return* after each line.

World Wide Web　　　　　A global online information source of interconnected data. Also called the *Web*.

BIBLIOGRAPHY

For additional help with your electronic or traditional writing, consider the following sources:

Angell, David, and Brent Heslop, *The Elements of E-mail Style: Communicate Effectively via Electronic Mail.* Reading, MA: Addison-Wesley Publishing Company, 1994.

Corbett, Edward, P. J., *The Little English Handbook: Choices and Conventions.* New York: John Wiley & Sons, 1977.

Hartman, Diane, B., and Karen S. Nantz, *The 3 Rs of E-Mail: Risks, Rights, and Responsibilities.* Menlo Park, CA: Crisp Publications, Inc., 1996.

Levine, John, R., Carol Baroudi, Margaret Levine Young, and Arnold Reinhold, *E-Mail For Dummies.* Foster City, CA: IDG Books Worldwide, Inc., 1997.

Microsoft Press Computer Dictionary. Redmond, WA: Microsoft Press, 1997.

Tarshis, Barry, *Grammar for Smart People.* New York: Pocket Books, 1992.

The American Heritage Dictionary. Ed. Anne H. Soukhanov. Boston, MA: Houghton Mifflin Company, 1992.

Williams, Joseph, M., *Style: Ten Lessons in Clarity & Grace.* Glenview, IL: Scott, Foresman and Company, 1981.

Wydick, Richard, C., *Plain English For Lawyers.* Durham, NC: Carolina Academic Press, 1994.

Wired Style: Principles of English Usage in the Digital Age. Ed. Constance Hale. San Francisco, CA: HardWired, 1996.

Look to the World Wide Web for additional information on e-mail, writing, and computers.

NOTES

NOTES

NOTES

NOTES

NOTES

Now Available From

Books • Videos • CD-ROMs • Computer-Based Training Products

Subject Areas Include:

Management

Human Resources

Communication Skills

Personal Development

Marketing/Sales

Organizational Development

Customer Service/Quality

Computer Skills

Small Business and Entrepreneurship

Adult Literacy and Learning

Life Planning and Retirement

CRISP WORLDWIDE DISTRIBUTION

English language books are distributed worldwide. Major international distributors include:

ASIA/PACIFIC

Australia/New Zealand: In Learning, PO Box 1051, Springwood QLD, Brisbane,
Australia 4127   Tel: 61-7-3-841-2286, Facsimile: 61-7-3-841-1580
ATTN: Messrs. Gordon

Philippines: National Book Store Inc., Quad Alpha Centrum Bldg, 125 Pioneer Street,
Mandaluyong, Metro Manila, Philippines   Tel: 632-631-8051, Facsimile: 632-631-5016

Singapore, Malaysia, Brunei, Indonesia: Times Book Shops. Direct sales HQ:
STP Distributors, Pasir Panjang Distrientre, Block 1 #03-01A, Pasir Panjang Rd,
Singapore 118480   Tel: 65-2767626, Facsimile: 65-2767119

Japan: Phoenix Associates Co., Ltd., Mizuho Bldng, 3-F, 2-12-2, Kami Osaki,
Shinagawa-Ku, Tokyo 141   Tel: 81-33-443-7231, Facsimile: 81-33-443-7640
ATTN: Mr. Peter Owans

CANADA

Crisp Learning Canada, 60 Briarwood Avenue, Mississauga, ON L5G 3N6 Canada
Tel: (905) 274-5678, Facsimile: (905) 278-2801
ATTN: Mr. Steve Connolly/Mr. Jerry McNabb

Trade Book Stores: Raincoast Books, 8680 Cambie Street,
Vancouver, BC V6P 6M9 Canada
Tel: (604) 323-7100, Facsimile: (604) 323-2600   ATTN: Order Desk

EUROPEAN UNION

England: Flex Training, Ltd., 9-15 Hitchin Street,
Baldock, Hertfordshire, SG7 6A, England
Tel: 44-1-46-289-6000, Facsimile: 44-1-46-289-2417   ATTN: Mr. David Willetts

INDIA

Multi-Media HRD, Pvt., Ltd., National House,
Tulloch Road, Appolo Bunder, Bombay, India 400-039
Tel: 91-22-204-2281, Facsimile: 91-22-283-6478   ATTN: Messrs. Aggarwal

SOUTH AMERICA

Mexico: Grupo Editorial Iberoamerica, Nebraska 199, Col. Napoles, 03810 Mexico, D.F.
Tel: 525-523-0994, Facsimile: 525-543-1173   ATTN: Señor Nicholas Grepe

SOUTH AFRICA

Alternative Books, PO Box 1345, Ferndale 2160, South Africa
Tel: 27-11-792-7730, Facsimile: 27-11-792-7787   ATTN: Mr. Vernon de Haas